# WIDE OPEN DOORS

*Wide Open Doors: Heaven's Favor for Opportunity, Influence, and Success*

Copyright © 2023 by Marilyn & Sarah Ministries

All rights reserved. No part of this book may be reproduced or transmitted in any form or by any means, electronic or mechanical, including photocopying, recording, or by any information storage and retrieval system, without permission in writing from the publisher.

Marilyn & Sarah Ministries
PO Box 6598
Englewood, CO 80155-6598
marilynandsarah.org

Edited by Bobbie Sartini, Nancy Buckner, and Sarah Heaton

ISBN 978-1-938696-31-2

Unless otherwise indicated, all Scripture quotations are taken from the New King James Version®. Copyright © 1982 by Thomas Nelson. Used by permission. All rights reserved.

Scripture quotations marked NIV are taken from the Holy Bible, New International Version®, NIV®. Copyright © 1973, 1978, 1984, 2011 by Biblica, Inc.™ Used by permission of Zondervan. All rights reserved worldwide. www.zondervan.com. The "NIV" and "New International Version" are trademarks registered in the United States Patent and Trademark Office by Biblica, Inc.™

Scripture quotations marked MEV are taken from the Modern English Version. Copyright © 2014 by Military Bible Association. Used by permission. All rights reserved.

Any bold typeface appearing in Scripture quotations have been added by the author.

Assembled and Produced for Marilyn & Sarah Ministries by
Breakfast for Seven
2150 E. Continental Blvd., Southlake, TX 76092
breakfastforseven.com

Printed in the United States of America.

# WIDE OPEN DOORS

Heaven's Favor for Opportunity, Influence, and Success

## MARILYN HICKEY

Marilyn & Sarah

# CONTENTS

A Note from Marilyn ........................................................................... vii

**CHAPTER ONE**
Favor for Your Family ........................................................................ 1

**CHAPTER TWO**
Favor for Your Health ...................................................................... 11

**CHAPTER THREE**
Favor for Your Nation ...................................................................... 17

**CHAPTER FOUR**
Favor for Your Circumstances ........................................................ 37

**CHAPTER FIVE**

The Principles of Godly Favor ............................................. 51

**CHAPTER SIX**

The Benefits of Godly Favor ............................................... 59

**APPENDIX A**

Prayer for Favor .................................................................. 73

**APPENDIX B**

Scriptures on Favor ............................................................. 85

End Notes ............................................................................ 91
Favor Forever ...................................................................... 93
About Marilyn Hickey ......................................................... 97
Learn more about Marilyn & Sarah Ministries ................. 101

# A NOTE FROM MARILYN

Are you looking for open doors of God's favor everywhere you turn? If not, you should. That's what He promises you in His Word!

I remember, many years ago, I asked the Lord if it was alright to pray to Him for favor in specific situations. Digging through His Word, I became thoroughly convinced that it was! Psalm 5:12 teaches, *"For You, O Lord, will bless the righteous; with favor You will surround him as with a shield."* This verse will be mentioned many times throughout this book, and I encourage you to become familiar with it. I was pleasantly surprised when I found out that the Hebrew word for "surround" in this passage means "crown." Second Corinthians 5:21 says, *"God made him (Jesus) who had no sin to be sin for us, so that in him we might become the **righteousness** of God"* (NIV, emphasis added). If you are a born-again, blood-bought child of the King, you're righteous, so envision a beautiful crown of favor on your head. Your crown of favor is also a shield, a wall of God's gracious favor, protecting you from anything that the enemy tries to bring against you!

Several years ago, I traveled to Sudan to hold healing meetings in a large public stadium there. We thought that we had successfully navigated all the political red tape and had full permission from the government, but about three hours before the first healing meeting was to start, we were told that a local bishop had turned against us. He had enough political influence to keep us from being able to hold the meetings. Shocked, we asked our contact at the stadium if that were true. "Yes, it's true. If he doesn't shut us down, it's an act of God!" Sadly, the man who wanted to shut us down was a fellow believer. We felt stuck. With no other choice, we decided to proceed as if the meeting was still being held that night. **As it turned out, the favor of God was greater than the** opposition. The vice president of Sudan arrived at the stadium and announced that the meeting could be held. We quickly discovered that his authority and God's power had more clout than the bishop's and his government connections. The vice president of Sudan attended the meetings every night, which gave us the ability to ignore the demands of those who stood against us.

That first night, 37,000 people attended, and we saw an amazing move of God that resulted in many people being healed, saved, and set free. The second and third nights, the crowd grew to 45,000 and then 54,000 people. By the final night, 65,000 people attended the meeting, and over 10,000 more, who were unable to get into the stadium, stood outside to listen from the street. Thousands of people were touched by the love and power of God that night. Over 20,000 received salvation, and many more experienced the miracle healing of God.

On any given day, security could be critical. In that city, violence often erupted without any warning or provocation. The normal threat of violence multiplied when we added several nights of growing attendance at extremely powerful Christian meetings. However, during our entire stay in Sudan, the Lord was with us. We made it through our time there without any incidents of violence.

God not only gave us favor with the government, but He also gave us favor with those who attended the meetings and surrounded us as a shield in a city that could be very dangerous.

I have story after story of God's miraculous favor at work in my life, and you'll read some of those in this book. But in addition to my own testimonies, we will look at some particularly favored people found in the Bible and the miracles and blessings God worked on their behalf. We'll also discuss some of the principles and benefits of favor, like purpose and provision. I believe that favor isn't just for people in the Bible, or those that preach on television. In Acts 10:34, Peter states: "... *God shows no partiality.*" God can open His doors of favor in your life just like He has for me and just like He did for those in the Bible whom we will read about in the following pages. Unleash the amazing abundance of His favor in your life, as well as in your family, your health, your circumstances, and even your nation!

CHAPTER ONE

# FAVOR FOR YOUR FAMILY

To me, Ruth is one of the sweetest books in the Bible. It's the eighth book of the Old Testament, and eight is the number of new beginnings. In this chapter, I want you to see how a family can be blessed with tremendous favor, despite how their story may have started.

At the beginning of the book of Ruth, it says there was a famine in Israel, and a man named Elimelech and his wife, Naomi, moved with their sons to the country of Moab. Over the course of 10 years, Elimelech died, the two sons married Moabite women, and then the sons died. After the deaths of her husband and two sons, Naomi decided to return to Israel, and she encouraged her daughters-in-law — Orpah and Ruth — to return home to their birth families:

> But Naomi said, "Turn back, my daughters; why will you go with me? Are there still sons in my womb, that they may be your husbands? Turn back, my daughters, go — for I am too old to have a husband. If I should say I have hope, if I should have a husband tonight and should also bear sons, would you wait for them till they were grown? Would you restrain yourselves from having husbands? No, my daughters; for it grieves me very much for your sakes that the hand of the LORD has gone out against me!"
>
> Then they lifted up their voices and wept again; and Orpah kissed her mother-in-law, but Ruth clung to her.
>
> And she said, "Look, your sister-in-law has gone back to her people and to her gods; return after your sister-in-law." (RUTH 1:11–15)

This is where the story of Ruth really begins. No matter how much Naomi implored her, Ruth refused to leave, saying:

> "*Entreat me not to leave you,*
> *Or to turn back from following after you;*
> *For wherever you go, I will go;*
> *And wherever you lodge, I will lodge;*
> *Your people shall be my people,*
> *And your God, my God.*
> *Where you die, I will die,*
> *And there will I be buried.*
> *The* L<small>ORD</small> *do so to me, and more also,*
> *If anything but death parts you and me.*"
> (RUTH 1:16–17)

Now, the Moabites were a cursed people, first, because they were born out of incest, and second, because they worshiped an idol called Chemosh. But when Ruth said to Naomi, "I want your God to be my God," the power of blessing came onto a family lineage that could have been very cursed. Ruth dropped her idolatry, the curse was broken, and the blessings of God were really upon her.

Ruth and Naomi ended up back in Bethlehem, but Naomi was very whiny. When the people call her "Naomi," she says, "Oh, don't call me Naomi, call me Mara, because God has dealt so bitterly with me" (Ruth 1:20). I think, *Lady, it wasn't God that made the decision to move to Moab. You and your husband made that decision, and you shouldn't have.* But isn't that how we are sometimes?

"Oh God, why did you do this?"

"Well, why did you make the wrong decision?"

So, Naomi was quite negative upon returning to Bethlehem, but they returned right at the time of the barley harvest, and Ruth went to glean in the fields after the harvesters. She ended up in the field of Boaz, who was related to Naomi's dead husband. When Boaz's servants told him about Ruth, he said to her:

> *"You will listen, my daughter, will you not?*
> *Do not go to glean in another field, nor go*
> *from here, but stay close by my young women.*
> *Let your eyes be on the field which they reap,*
> *and go after them. Have I not commanded the*

*young men not to touch you? And when you are thirsty, go to the vessels and drink from what the young men have drawn."*

*So she fell on her face, bowed down to the ground, and said to him, "Why have I found favor in your eyes, that you should take notice of me, since I am a foreigner?"*

*And Boaz answered and said to her, "It has been fully reported to me, all that you have done for your mother-in-law since the death of your husband, and how you have left your father and your mother and the land of your birth, and have come to a people whom you did not know before. The* Lord *repay your work, and a full reward be given you by the* Lord *God of Israel, under whose wings you have come for refuge."*

*Then she said, "Let me find favor in your sight, my lord; for you have comforted me, and have spoken kindly to your maidservant, though I am not like one of your maidservants."*

*Now Boaz said to her at mealtime, "Come here, and eat of the bread, and dip your piece of bread in the vinegar." So she sat beside the reapers, and he passed parched grain to her; and she ate and was satisfied, and kept some back. And when she rose up to glean, Boaz commanded his young men, saying, "Let her glean even among the sheaves, and do not reproach her. Also let grain from the bundles fall purposely for her; leave it that she may glean, and do not rebuke her."* (RUTH 2:8–16)

This is the first place where we really see the favor of God on Ruth. Boaz gives her food, water, and a safe place to glean. Then, in chapter three, Naomi tells Ruth to meet Boaz at the threshing floor, lay at his feet, and ask him to be her kinsman-redeemer. Here, her favor increases even more with Boaz, and he says:

*"Blessed are you of the LORD, my daughter! For you have shown more kindness at the end than at the beginning, in that you did not go after young men, whether poor or rich. And now, my daughter, do not fear. I will do for you all that you request, for all the people of my town know that you are a virtuous woman. Now it is true that I am a close relative; however, there is a relative closer than I. Stay this night, and in the morning it shall be that if he will perform the duty of a close relative for you — good; let him do it. But if he does not want to perform the duty for you, then I will perform the duty for you, as the LORD lives! Lie down until morning."* (RUTH 3:10–13)

Becoming a kinsman-redeemer was quite a thing for a man to do. First, he had to take the widow, in this case Ruth, to be his wife. Then, he had to have enough money to buy the land that would belong to her family and pay off any debts that were owed. Finally, their children would have to bear the name of her deceased husband. A lot of men wouldn't have wanted to do this. But Ruth had favor with Boaz, and he took her as his wife.

In Ruth 4:11–12, all of the people who were there said, "*We are witnesses. The* LORD *make the woman who is coming to your house like Rachel and Leah, the two who built the house of Israel; and may you prosper in Ephrathah and be famous in Bethlehem. May your house be like the house of Perez, whom Tamar bore to Judah, because of the offspring which the* LORD *will give you from this young woman.*"

This transaction was a very spiritual thing. These witnesses understood that this was not just a man buying some land that belonged to a dead relative. They also understood that this was not just a man taking a wife and making a promise that he would raise up seed in the dead relative's name. They understood that they were to bless that home and the family lineage that would come out of it with favor. I want you to look again at verses 11 and 12.

"*The* LORD *make the woman who is coming to your house like Rachel and Leah, the two who built the house of Israel. . . . May your house be like the house of Perez, whom Tamar bore to Judah . . .*" (vv. 11–12). Now wait a minute.

Rachel and Leah bore the 12 sons that became the 12 tribes of Israel. It would be out of their household, the tribe of Judah in fact, that the Messiah would come. Now how can Ruth be blessed like that? She's a Moabite. She's not in that lineage. But they said, "Bless her so that her lineage will be like Rachel, Leah, and Tamar."

> **Did you know that you also have a kinsman-redeemer? Jesus Christ. He came in the flesh to redeem us, he paid for our debts on the cross, and he became our bridegroom.**

Ruth and Boaz had a son who was the grandfather of King David. But that's not the end of it. Ruth shows up in the genealogy of Jesus Christ in Matthew 1:5. Where did it start? With Ruth refusing to leave Naomi, and committing herself to Yahweh, the Hebrew God. Ruth took care of her mother-in-law and submitted herself not just to the authority of God but also to Naomi's authority when she impressed upon Ruth the need for Boaz to become their kinsman-redeemer.

Finally, when the witnesses blessed Ruth and Boaz, they blessed the entire household, and there was favor upon the family line.

Did you know that you also have a kinsman-redeemer? Jesus Christ. He came in the flesh to redeem us, he paid for our debts on the cross, and he became our bridegroom. When we become the bride of Jesus Christ, we become co-heirs with Him, and His blessings come to us. And we pass that on to our spouses, children, grandchildren, and great-grandchildren. Talk about favor!

Remember how I mentioned that the book of Ruth is the eighth book in the Bible, and eight is the number of new beginnings? Well, I believe that reading this book and putting into practice what you will learn is a new beginning of favor for you and your family that will last for generations!

CHAPTER TWO

# FAVOR FOR YOUR HEALTH

In 2 Kings 5, we find the story of a man, a valiant soldier, who was in a completely unfavorable health circumstance — he had leprosy. Yet, there was a young girl who found favor with this man, and her favor not only transformed his life but many other situations as well.

The man's name was Naaman. He was a brave, successful commanding general in the Syrian army. During one of Syria's raids, they had taken a young Israelite girl captive, and she became a servant to Naaman's wife. The Bible never tells us her name, but we do know that someone had planted the Word of God into her heart when she was very young. Even in captivity, she held fast to the Word and shared it with others. In spite of her circumstances, this girl found favor with God because she confidently witnessed His Word and allowed the truth to remain in her.

For her young age, she had a good understanding of Naaman's suffering and his needs. One day, she told Naaman's wife that he should visit the prophet Elisha in order to receive healing for his leprosy. When Naaman heard the suggestion, he gathered much wealth and brought it with him on his journey to Israel.

**Naaman wasn't thrilled with the prospect of washing himself in the Jordan seven times. When he heard Elisha's prescription for his condition, he was disgusted.**

When Naaman first arrived in the land, he presented a letter written by the king of Syria to the king of Israel. This letter announced that he was sending Naaman to Israel to be healed. The king of Syria really put the king of Israel on the spot! The Israelite king heatedly replied by saying, *"Am I God, to kill and make alive, that this man sends a man to me to heal him of his leprosy? Therefore please consider, and see how he seeks a quarrel with me"* (2 Kings 5:7).

Seeing that the king's situation was far different from that of the young maid's, I thought that it was interesting to note that she had more compassion for Naaman's circumstances than the king did! She realized the source for his healing was God's power, whereas the king didn't. Furthermore, the king of Israel lacked understanding, mercy, and truth, so Naaman was wasting his time trying to find favor with him!

Hearing that the king responded to Naaman by tearing his clothes over the situation, Elisha sent a messenger to Naaman, saying, *"Go and wash in the Jordan seven times, and your flesh shall be restored to you, and you shall be clean"* (2 Kings 5:10). Naaman wasn't thrilled with the prospect of washing himself in the Jordan seven times. When he heard Elisha's prescription for his condition, he was disgusted. What did Naaman expect Elisha to do? The Bible says:

> *Naaman became furious, and went away and said, "Indeed, I said to myself, 'He will surely*

*come out to me, and stand and call on the name of the* Lord *his God, and wave his hand over the place, and heal the leprosy.'"* (2 KINGS 5:11)

It is interesting to note the important roles which the servants played in this story. First, we see that Naaman's servant girl told him to go to Israel to seek his healing. Naaman would have left Israel enraged by his anger had not his other servants encouraged him to follow the prophet's advice: *"My father, if the prophet had told you to do something great, would you not have done it? How much more then, when he says to you, 'Wash, and be clean'?"* (2 Kings 5:13).

Naaman followed their encouragement and acted on Elisha's word: *"So he went down and dipped seven times in the Jordan, according to the saying of the man of God; and his flesh was restored like the flesh of a little child, and he was clean"* (2 Kings 5:14).

There was a reason why Naaman had favor in the sight of the Lord. God's promise to Abraham was: *"I will bless those who bless you, and I will curse him who curses you; and in you all the families of the earth shall be blessed"* (Genesis 12:3). This promise not only applied to Abraham, but it also applied to his seed.

The young servant girl was the seed of Abraham. We can surmise that Naaman must have been a very good master to his servants because in verse 13 they affectionately called him "Father" and they earnestly desired to see him healed. Even though she was a captive, I believe Naaman's kindness to the Jewish girl gave him favor in the sight of the Lord, and this favor led to his physical and spiritual healing.

> **Healing and salvation are often found together throughout the Bible. We hardly ever see them separated.**

After Naaman's miraculous healing, he returned to Elisha, and with much gratitude, he tried to persuade him to accept the treasure which he had brought, but Elisha refused. According to verses 18–19, we see that Naaman repented of his idolatrous past and was forgiven of his sins. After he was healed and forgiven, he asked Elisha for some dirt because he wanted to take it back to his home in Syria, where he planned to kneel on it and worship the God of the Jews. He was really touched by his healing, wasn't he? He abandoned the worship of Rimmon, the god of Babylon, and he learned to worship Jehovah, the true and living God!

Healing and salvation are often found together throughout the Bible. We hardly ever see them separated. Naaman's entire life was transformed through his encounter with God, which brought about his physical and spiritual healings. Both ancient history and the Bible agree that Syria attacked Israel many times after this incident, but there is no indication that Naaman ever led the Syrian army in battle against Israel after his miraculous healing. Isn't it wonderful how God touches us as individuals in order to place us in the path of His divine will? Once God puts His finger on your life, you're not only transformed, but the consequences of His divine touch are also often quite far-reaching, as they were in the case of Naaman.

Do you want favor for healing that will go beyond just your own body and circumstances and change the course of history as well? Nothing is too big for God!

## CHAPTER THREE

# FAVOR FOR YOUR NATION

Esther lived in a historically dark time. Following the Persian Empire's destruction of Babylon, many Jews had been displaced to Persia. Their king, Ahasuerus, ruled a kingdom of 127 provinces extending from India to Ethiopia. He was extremely wealthy and very astute in worldly matters.

As a demonstration of his worldly wealth, Ahasuerus called all the leaders of his provinces together for a six-month celebration. Can you imagine holding a six-month party? Talk about guests who made themselves at home! After these six months, he held a seven-day feast for everyone in the palace. The palace was elaborately decorated with gold and silver. Even the wine was served in golden vessels, each differing from the next. It was one of the most extravagant celebrations the world has ever known.

During that time in history, it was not customary for men and women to mingle at feasts. Therefore, Ahasuerus's queen, Vashti, hosted a special feast elsewhere in the palace for the women.

During the feast, the king became drunk with wine and bragged about what a knock-out his queen was, and sent word for Vashti to come into the court so that he could show her off. Some historians and Bible commentators say that he asked her to come in and expose herself indecently. *"But Queen Vashti refused to come at the king's command brought by his eunuchs; therefore the king was furious, and his anger burned within him"* (Esther 1:12). Vashti had the guts to exercise some class and say, "I'm a human being, and I refuse to be exhibited like one of your golden vessels."

Ahasuerus consulted his seven princely "wise men" about Vashti's behavior. One wise man, Memucan, was particularly upset with Vashti. My guess is that Memucan was henpecked at home, and he probably thought this was a great opportunity to take out his frustration on women. He advised the king, "You had better handle this woman because she's too gutsy. If you let her get away with this, all the women in the empire are going to rebel against their husbands. They won't cook meals, wash the clothes, or take care of the children! You have got to do something about her!" Memucan then recommended that the king divorce Vashti, saying:

> *"If it pleases the king, let a royal decree go out from him, and let it be recorded in the laws of the Persians and the Medes, so that it will not be altered, that Vashti shall come no more before King Ahasuerus; and let the king give her royal position to another who is better than she."*
> (ESTHER 1:19)

In a moment of anger, King Ahasuerus took Memucan's advice and deposed Vashti. But he soon realized that he had made a big mistake because he truly loved her. Unfortunately, it was too late. In those days, the king's laws couldn't be retracted.

After the wrath of King Ahasuerus subsided, he remembered Vashti and what had been decreed against her. In an effort to cheer him, the king's servants suggested that he hold a beauty contest in which all the beautiful women in his empire could participate. The servants said, "Surely there is a woman in your vast empire who could become a suitable queen." The king eagerly agreed to hold the contest.

**For one full year, all the beauty contestants were groomed and trained in a manner appropriate for a queen.**

Esther was a young Jewish girl who lived near the palace. Evidently, her family had been killed during the first Babylonian invasion, and she had been adopted by her cousin Mordecai, who was raising her as his own daughter. Mordecai and Esther were both captured during the second Babylonian invasion and exiled to Persia. While in Persia, Mordecai changed Esther's name from Hadassah to disguise her ancestry. He gave her the Persian name Esther, meaning "star." I think her new name really fit her. Like a star, Esther allowed the light of God to shine through her to penetrate a very dark generation.

However, Mordecai and Esther started out on the wrong foot. The prophet Jeremiah had instructed the Jews to return to Jerusalem after their 70-year captivity, but most refused. Only 60,000 Jews had chosen to return. The rest — over 2 million — decided to remain in Persian territory, including Mordecai and Esther. Besides that, Mordecai decided to enter Esther into the king's beauty contest, which wasn't a very holy thing to do. If she didn't win, she would automatically become a concubine to the king!

For one full year, all the beauty contestants were groomed and trained in a manner appropriate for a queen. At the end of the year, they were presented to the king one by one. When Esther went before the king, the Bible says, *"The king loved Esther more than all the other women, and she obtained grace and favor in his sight more than all the virgins; so he set the royal crown upon her head and made her queen instead of Vashti"* (Esther 2:17).

Esther delighted the king, and she was chosen to be his queen. Remember, the king loved to eat, so he held a great feast in Esther's honor. He also *"proclaimed a holiday in the provinces and gave gifts according to the generosity of a king"* (v. 18). All to celebrate the beautiful new wife he had chosen.

Do you think that God ordained this marriage? From our natural viewpoint, the union between a Jewess and a rich, materialistic, heathen king doesn't appear to be a match made in heaven. But remember, God is a God of providence. Providence means forethought of care and supply. God provided Esther with special access to an ungodly king so that she could divert her generation from impending destruction. God's providence is evident throughout the entire book of Esther. But I want to point out a very strange fact: God's name is not mentioned even once in this book! Although no one mentions God during this entire time period, He is present to move and guide the course of events that occur. Occasionally, it appears that God's people have forgotten Him, but He never forgets His people. He is still a God who can provide needed help. He is always a God of providence.

One day, Mordecai overheard two of the king's doorkeepers scheming to kill the king. Evil plots were nothing new in those days — nor in our day. Mordecai sent an urgent message to Esther, and

Esther informed the king, giving credit to Mordecai. The two doorkeepers were executed, and the plot was squelched.

What was done to reward Mordecai? Initially, nothing. No one said, "Oh, Mordecai, you're such a hero!" Have you ever done something that went completely unnoticed or maybe even backfired? Maybe you thought, *No good deed goes unpunished! It's not worth it.* Believe me, if you stay true to God, then His hand will be in your situation. Eventually, you will reap what you sow. Galatians 6:9 says, *"Let us not grow weary while doing good, for in due season we shall reap if we do not lose heart."*

> **The sons of Esau hated the sons of Jacob, and this went on for centuries. So we have a generational curse: antisemitism.**

It seems as though there's a villain in every story, and Esther's is no different. In Esther 3:1, Ahasuerus promoted a very ungodly man, Haman, to the number-one position in the kingdom. Haman, as the highest of the king's princes, was consumed with pride. He loved his position in the Persian Empire. Haman, however, was not a Persian, he was an Agagite, which means he was of Amalekite descent. Why does this matter? Well, the Amalekites were descendants of the Edomites, and the Edomites were descended from Esau. The sons of Esau hated the sons of Jacob, and this went on for centuries. So we have a generational curse: antisemitism. This isn't a new thing, and it's satanic. It's the devil's plan.

Now, Haman's position required everyone to bow down to him when he passed on the street. No one dared to defy Haman! But Mordecai refused to bow — I think he saw right through Haman all along. The king's servants tried to get Mordecai to bow down, but Mordecai stood firm. Now watch God move on Mordecai's behalf . . .

Haman was furious with Mordecai. Mordecai had suddenly come out of his quiet corner and taken a daring stand against Haman. What a blow to Haman's ego! Although he was enraged, Haman was afraid to confront Mordecai directly. So Haman went to the king and said:

> *"There is a certain people scattered and dispersed among the people in all the provinces of your kingdom; their laws are different from all other people's, and they do not keep the king's laws. Therefore it is not fitting for the king to let them remain. If it pleases the king, let a decree be written that they be destroyed, and I will pay ten thousand talents of silver into the hands of those who do the work, to bring it into the king's treasuries."*
>
> *So the king took his signet ring from his hand and gave it to Haman, the son of Hammedatha the Agagite, the enemy of the Jews. And the king said to Haman, "The money and the people are given to you, to do with them as seems good to you."*
>
> (ESTHER 3:8–11)

The king signed Haman's decree, which proclaimed that all the Jews were to be killed. The decree was translated into all the languages of the provinces, and messengers were sent out to proclaim that all the Jews, both young and old, would be killed. Remember, no one except Mordecai knew Esther was

Jewish. Since she was secluded in the palace, she was in a real predicament and didn't even know it. She was included in the death decree, and the law of a Persian king couldn't be altered once it was passed.

When Mordecai heard the decree, he put on sackcloth and ashes and began to weep in front of the palace gate. Someone went to Esther and said, "Your cousin is outside crying. He looks awful. He's wearing sackcloth and ashes!" (Esther 4:4).

**When we surrender ourselves to God, it brings favor. It's not easy, and we usually have to surrender more than once.**

Esther did what many women do when they hear bad news — she went shopping! Esther bought Mordecai a brand-new outfit and sent a messenger to tell him to take off his sackcloth and ashes. She probably thought that new clothes would help cheer him up. But Mordecai told the messenger, "Send the outfit back to Esther and let her know that we are in a very serious situation. The king has signed a decree to kill all the Jews. Plead to the king on our behalf."

But Esther hesitated. The king hadn't called for her in over 30 days, which very well could have meant that she had fallen out of favor with him. There was a law among the Persian kings that if you went into the court and the king didn't extend his golden scepter to you, you would be executed. Even though she was the queen, Esther could die if she went before the king without being summoned by him. But Mordecai wouldn't take no for an answer:

> *"Do not think in your heart that you will escape in the king's palace any more than all the other Jews. For if you remain completely silent at this time, relief and deliverance will arise for the Jews from another place, but you and your father's house will perish. Yet who knows whether you have come to the kingdom for such a time as this?"* (ESTHER 4:13–14)

Esther's response is the key to our favor: "... *I will go to the king, which is against the law; and if I perish, I perish!*" (Esther 4:16). Why is this the key? Because she surrenders her will to the will of God. When we surrender ourselves to God, it brings favor. It's not easy, and we usually have to surrender more than once. In fact, we usually end up having to surrender over and over again! But when we surrender and lay down our life, that's when God shows up!

> **The future looked pretty bleak for Esther's cousin, but remember, God is a God of providence. Whenever His children call on His name, He will move heaven and earth to protect them.**

God gave Esther a plan, and she told Mordecai to gather a group of Jews to fast with her for three days; then she would go in to see the king, even if she ended up being executed for breaking the law. This young Jewish maiden made a commitment to trust God and allow Him to use her in His divine plan to rescue the entire Jewish nation. When you surrender to God, He gives you His favor. When you have favor with God, He gives you favor with man, and that's exactly what happened with Esther. After the Jews had fasted and prayed, Esther went to see the king:

*So it was, when the king saw Queen Esther standing in the court, that she found favor in his sight, and the king held out to Esther the golden scepter that was in his hand. Then Esther went near and touched the top of the scepter.*

*And the king said to her, "What do you wish, Queen Esther? What is your request? It shall be given to you — up to half the kingdom!"*
(ESTHER 5:2–3)

God again gave Esther favor with the king. Esther thought it would be wise to ease into the request and maybe butter the king up a little bit, so she replied, "I just wanted to ask you and Haman to come to dinner tonight."

That evening at dinner, the king was so enamored by Esther that he said to her again, "Ask whatever you like. I will give you up to half of my kingdom!" Esther responded with a second dinner invitation for the next evening, promising the king that she would then give him her request.

Haman must have really thought he had it made now that he had been invited to two of the queen's dinner parties. Little did he know that the next banquet would be a "necktie" party and he would be the guest of honor. Haman told his wife Zeresh, "I love my life, and I just love my job. The only flaw is Mordecai, the man at the gate who won't bow to me."

Zeresh exclaimed, "I have an idea! Build tall gallows and hang Mordecai from it. That will take care of him!"

> **No situation is impossible for God. He can interrupt the devil's plans and change a curse into a blessing.**

Haman leaped at his wife's suggestion. He wanted revenge so badly that he ordered his men to build gallows 75 feet high just to kill Mordecai (Esther 5:9–14). Why did Haman build such tall gallows? I think He wanted to make a big example out of Mordecai! The future looked pretty bleak for Esther's cousin, but remember, God is a God of providence. Whenever His children call on His name, He will move heaven and earth to protect them.

The Bible says that pride always precedes a fall (Proverbs 16:18). Haman was ensnared in a tremendous web of pride, and he was about to plunge into disaster. After Haman had the gallows built, King Ahasuerus had a sleepless night. Who do you think was keeping the king awake? God. He used a simple little thing like sleep to change the course of history.

After tossing and turning for a while, the king finally gave into his insomnia and decided to get some work done. He asked his servants to read to him from the book which contained everyone's name who had blessed the king. *"And it was found written that Mordecai had told of Bigthana and Teresh, two of the king's eunuchs, the doorkeepers who had sought to lay hands on King Ahasuerus"* (Esther 6:2).

The king asked his servants, "Mordecai saved my life. Has he ever been rewarded for his noble deed?"

"Nothing has been done for him," they replied.

Now, Haman had just walked into the court to speak with the king about hanging Mordecai, but before he was given an opportunity, the king asked him, "Haman, what could I do to honor a man who has been especially good to me?"

Thinking that he was the one to be honored, Haman replied:

> "For the man whom the king delights to honor, let a royal robe be brought which the king has worn, and a horse on which the king has ridden, which has a royal crest placed on its head. Then let this robe and horse be delivered to the hand of one of the king's most noble princes, that he may array the man whom the king delights to honor. Then parade him on horseback through the city square, and proclaim before him: 'Thus shall it be done to the man whom the king delights to honor!'"
>
> (ESTHER 6:7–9)

Haman pictured himself wearing the king's beautiful robes and parading through the streets on the king's horse, while everyone — including Mordecai — bowed down to him.

But before Haman could ask the king, "Who is to be honored?"

The king said, "*Hurry, take the robe and the horse, as you have suggested, and do so for Mordecai the Jew who sits within the king's gate! Leave nothing undone of all that you have spoken*" (Esther 6:10).

Haman was greatly disappointed. After he had fulfilled the king's wishes and paraded Mordecai through town, Haman rushed home to tell his wife and friends what had happened. They became frightened and said: *"If Mordecai, before whom you have begun to fall, is of Jewish descent, you will not prevail against him but will surely fall before him"* (Esther 6:13).

**Just as God enabled Esther to become a woman of favor and thwart Haman's plot against the Jews, God can enable you to halt ungodly forces against your family, community, and nation.**

No situation is impossible for God. He can interrupt the devil's plans and change a curse into a blessing. Watch how God reversed the devil's plot to annihilate the Jews.

At Esther's second banquet, the king must have been on pins and needles, wondering what Esther could possibly want. Finally, she made her request, "My people have been condemned to death, and I want them to be saved."

Realizing that he had signed his own wife's death warrant, the king became so upset that he went for a walk in the palace garden. Haman knew he was in big trouble, so he ran over to the couch upon which Esther was reclining and began to beg for his life. Upon his return to the banquet room, the king saw Haman had fallen over Esther on the couch and yelled, *"Will he also assault the queen while I am in the house?"* (Esther 7:8).

One would think that nothing more could go wrong for Haman, but, in reality, his trouble was just beginning. He was taken back to his house not in honor but as a condemned prisoner. Not wanting such fine workmanship to go to waste, the king sentenced Haman to die on his own gallows. Then he gave over to Esther the property of Haman, and she appointed Mordecai to oversee it (Esther 7:9–8:2).

In the meantime, the Jews were still sentenced to death. So, Esther approached the king and pleaded with him on their behalf. King Ahasuerus answered her and Mordecai by saying:

> *"You yourselves write a decree concerning the Jews, as you please, in the king's name, and seal it with the king's signet ring; for whatever is written in the king's name and sealed with the king's signet ring no one can revoke."*
> (ESTHER 8:8)

Talk about favor! Mordecai and Esther called in the scribes and wrote a letter permitting *"the Jews who were in every city to gather together and protect their lives — to destroy, kill, and annihilate all the forces of any people or province that would assault them"* (Esther 8:11). The chapter finishes by saying:

> *The Jews had light and gladness, joy and honor. And in every province and city, wherever the king's command and decree came, the Jews had joy and gladness, a feast and a holiday. Then many of the people of the land became Jews, because fear of the Jews fell upon them.*
> (ESTHER 8:16–17)

The book of Esther beautifully illustrates how God transforms seemingly average people into glorious vessels that he can use to penetrate dark and sinful times. Just as God enabled Esther to become a woman of favor and thwart Haman's plot against the Jews, God can enable you to halt ungodly forces against your family, community, and nation.

God didn't look at Esther in the natural realm and declare, "She has a beautiful face, so I can use her." Or "Esther had a 4.0 grade point average in high school, so she's smart enough to change the course of her nation." You can make a significant difference in the world around you. Like Esther, you were created *"for such a time as this."* But also like Esther, you must lay down your will and say, *"If I perish, I perish."* God desires our surrender and willingness to follow His guidance. Satan is powerless against a believer who has the favor of the Lord on their side. Don't hesitate to call on the name of Jesus and stand on God's Word to overcome circumstances and change your nation.

God wants to use you in His providence during this time on the earth, and His hand is on you in a supernatural way!

CHAPTER FOUR

## FAVOR FOR YOUR CIRCUMSTANCES

There is an unusual love story found in 1 Samuel, and I want to show you how favor played an important key in the development of this story. This story skillfully intertwines the lives of three people: David, a fugitive from King Saul; Nabal, a wealthy but cantankerous husband; and Abigail, Nabal's beautiful, wise, and industrious wife. Now, before I begin, I'm going to give you a brief background of our three leading characters.

Our story is found in 1 Samuel, chapter 25. In this episode of David's life, he was running from King Saul, who was trying to kill him. In the previous chapter, Saul had taken 3,000 men in pursuit of David and his men. During the pursuit, the Lord purposely delivered Saul into David's hands to do what seemed good to him (v. 4). It sounds like a beautiful chance for David to get even with Saul, doesn't it? Some of us would like God to give us an opportunity similar to the one that He gave David, wouldn't we? Do you think that most of us would be motivated to respond to the occasion in the Spirit or in the flesh? Let's see what David did . . .

David found Saul in a cave, and he secretly crept in and cautiously cut the corner off of Saul's robe! Don't you think that Saul must have been more than a little embarrassed when he found out about David's trick? He sure was! But you can believe that he was grateful to David for sparing his life and leaving him unharmed. Because David had not taken this golden opportunity to kill Saul, he showed his true spiritual stature, and even Saul recognized it. Saul acknowledged that David would be Israel's king, and that the kingdom of Israel would be established in his hand (v. 20). Saul instinctively knew that David had proved his righteousness by the manner in which David had responded to the opportunity of getting even with him. Saul knew that the Lord was going to grant David favor and firmly establish the kingdom in David's hands by making him king.

Our next episode of the story finds David in the wilderness, in a dry place called Paran. David and his men began to suffer from hunger, so he sought assistance and food from a wealthy man named Nabal.

Nabal, whose name means "folly," was notorious for his ugly disposition. Nabal couldn't blame his churlish disposition on his ancestors, for he was a descendant of Caleb, one of the two spies who gave Moses a "good report" concerning the land of Canaan. Because Caleb and another spy, Joshua, had positive attitudes and didn't murmur against the Lord about the land that He had prepared for the children of Israel, they were the only two men who were still alive 40 years later out of the original hundreds of thousands who had left Egypt with them! When the children of Israel finally entered the promised land, Caleb claimed Hebron, the mountain which God had promised him 40 years earlier. Hebron was a land occupied by giants. One would have thought that Caleb, a man over 80 years old, would have been too tired, old, and weak to have fought for a land inhabited by giants, but he didn't even need to enter into combat. Joshua 11:23 tells us that *"the land rested from war."* The Hebrew word "rest" in this passage can mean to be quiet or still. I think that when the giants heard of the reputation of Caleb, they just decided to be quiet, and therefore he didn't even need to raise his hand in battle to take their land! God showed favor to Caleb because he was willing to take God at His Word despite existing obstacles. He was a man of faith, unlike his later descendant, Nabal.

Since the land of Hebron was Nabal's inheritance from his ancestor, Caleb, Nabal couldn't blame his ugly disposition on the fact that he had to work day and night to acquire his land. He was just reaping an unmerited inheritance. Nabal also had a lovely wife by the name of Abigail, and she is described as *"a woman of good understanding and beautiful appearance"* (1 Samuel 25:3). It is apparent that Nabal had been richly blessed by God in all areas of his life and had no excuse for his obnoxious, arrogant behavior!

Now, while David and his men were in the wilderness, they had protected Nabal's shepherds and his flocks of sheep. So when he and his men grew hungry, David sent 10 of his young men out to ask Nabal to give them food. David desired to find favor with

Nabal, therefore he coached his men on what they would say to him. His young men were told to bless Nabal by saying:

> *"Peace be to you, peace to your house, and peace to all that you have! Now I have heard that you have shearers. Your shepherds were with us, and we did not hurt them, nor was there anything missing from them all the while they were in Carmel. Ask your young men, and they will tell you. Therefore let my young men find favor in your eyes, for we come on a feast day. Please give whatever comes to your hand to your servants and to your son David."*
>
> (1 SAMUEL: 25:6–8)

When David's men gave Nabal this message, he belligerently answered them by saying:

> *"Who is David, and who is the son of Jesse? There are many servants nowadays who break away each one from his master. Shall **I** then take **my** bread and **my** water and **my** meat that*

*I have killed for **my** shearers, and give it to men when **I** do not know where they are from?"*
(1 SAMUEL 25:10–11, EMPHASIS ADDED)

Did you notice Nabal's self-centered response to David's plea for help? Every other word out of his mouth was "my" or "I"! You didn't hear him give God the glory for his wealth, did you? Psalm 14:1 teaches:

*The fool has said in his heart,*
*"There is no God."*
*They are corrupt,*
*They have done abominable works,*
*There is none who does good.*

Nabal's inconsiderate actions showed that he was acting the part of a fool and fulfilling the meaning of his name!

When David heard his men recount Nabal's answer to them, he irrationally responded in anger by saying to his men:

> *"Every man gird on his sword. . . . Surely in vain I have protected all that this fellow has in the wilderness, so that nothing was missed of all that belongs to him. And he has repaid me evil for good. May God do so, and more also, to the enemies of David, if I leave one male of all who belong to him by morning light."*
>
> (1 SAMUEL 25:13, 21–22)

You can see that David was absolutely enraged! We must always be careful how we react to another's nasty disposition. From the very beginning of Saul's pursuit of David, David remained an example of level-headed faith. He had previously had two opportunities to kill Saul, but because he trusted God, he passed up the chances. But now, a minor incident triggered David's anger to the point that he not only wanted to kill Nabal, but he also intended to include Nabal's entire household as well. By recklessly responding to the annoying situation at hand, David would have been responsible for shedding innocent blood.

Why is it that we can make it through some pretty big ordeals, but a minor incident happens, and our mind blows it out of proportion, and we respond by

EXPLODING! Do you know why this happens? It is because we rely solely on our own sense-knowledge rather than faith. Our senses will always encourage us to take a one-sided, distorted view of reality and therefore prompt us to make rash decisions which we later regret. Faith always tells us to proceed calmly, and it helps us to rest in the assurance that we will have favor in any trying situation, despite negative appearances.

Upon hearing Nabal's refusal to give David food, Abigail acted in wisdom. She responded to the crisis by acting in faith! In confidence, one of Abigail's young men told her about Nabal's refusal to feed David and his men. Abigail's servant realized that she was aware of the fact that David had protected Nabal's servants and sheep, so he wanted to warn her that her home was in danger. When Abigail heard the young man's report, she did a very spiritual thing: She hastily prepared a feast for David and his men. The Bible tells us that *"the wise woman builds her house"* (Proverbs 14:1). By responding to the trying situation in faith and love, Abigail did just that! (1 Samuel 25:14–19).

Abigail set out to meet David, and when she saw him, she quickly got off of her donkey and fell before David on her face. Abigail gave David a soft answer, and by doing so, she turned his wrath away from her house (see Proverbs 15:1). Let's look at what she said:

> "On me, my lord, on me let this iniquity be! And please let your maidservant speak in your ears, and hear the words of your maidservant. Please, let not my lord regard this scoundrel Nabal. For as his name is, so is he: Nabal is his name, and folly is with him! But I, your maidservant, did not see the young men of my lord whom you sent. Now therefore, my lord, as the LORD lives and as your soul lives, since the LORD has held you back from coming to bloodshed and from avenging yourself with your own hand, now then, let your enemies and those who seek harm for my lord be as Nabal. And now this present which your maidservant has brought to my lord, let it be given to the young men who follow my lord. Please forgive the trespass of your maidservant. For the LORD will certainly make for my lord an enduring house, because my lord fights the battles of the LORD, and evil is not found in you throughout your days. Yet a man has risen to pursue you and seek your life, but the life of my lord shall be bound in the bundle of

*the living with the* LORD *your God; and the lives of your enemies He shall sling out, as from the pocket of a sling. And it shall come to pass, when the* LORD *has done for my lord according to all the good that He has spoken concerning you, and has appointed you ruler over Israel, that this will be no grief to you, nor offense of heart to my lord, either that you have shed blood without cause, or that my lord has avenged himself. But when the* LORD *has dealt well with my lord, then remember your maidservant."*

*Then David said to Abigail: "Blessed is the* LORD *God of Israel, who sent you this day to meet me! And blessed is your advice and blessed are you, because you have kept me this day from coming to bloodshed and from avenging myself with my own hand. For indeed, as the* LORD *God of Israel lives, who has kept me back from hurting you, unless you had hurried and come to meet me, surely by morning light no males would have been left to Nabal!"*

(1 SAMUEL 25:24–34)

Abigail was a good wife. She didn't say to David, "You see how rotten my husband behaved. Positively no one can live with him. Go ahead and kill him! You'll make me a rich widow." No! She freely admitted to David that her husband had acted like a fool, but she humbly said, *"On me let this iniquity be."*

David initially asked for favor from Nabal, but he found it instead with Abigail. Favor may not always come in the way which we think it should, but if we claim it, we will receive our expected blessing. God's Word will not fail. Psalm 5:12 says: *"For You, O Lord, will bless the righteous; with favor You will surround him as with a shield."* God did not let His servant follow his natural impulses, which were motivated by anger. Instead, God purposely brought the favor of Abigail to David, and a situation was avoided which would have definitely ended in murder.

I think 1 Samuel 25:29 is one of the most profound verses in the Bible. Abigail lifted up the discouraged David by saying, *"The life of my lord shall be bound in the bundle of the living with the Lord your God."* Do you realize that your soul — which consists of your mind, will, and emotions — is ingeniously bound in a bundle of supernatural life and power with God?

What was Abigail telling David? She was warning him: "Be careful, David! Don't shed innocent blood. If you do, you will be untying your bundle of life." Do you know what happens when this intricate bundle is unwrapped? Death worms its way into the circumstances of your life, and you lose the blessings and the protection of the Lord.

> **God knows how to take care of our enemies . . .**

What a beautiful spirit resided in Abigail! When David walked into her favor, he really walked into something! Abigail requested that David remember her when the Lord fulfilled the promise of making him ruler over Israel. David not only accepted Abigail's food, but he also accepted her advice as well, because he realized that it was blessed and inspired by the Lord. David returned Abigail's blessing by saying, *"Go up in peace to your house. See, I have heeded your voice and respected your person"* (1 Samuel 25:35).

How did God's blessing of favor help David through his encounter with Abigail? She gave him food to nourish his body, but most of all, she encouraged him, lifted him up in his spirit, and fed his hungry soul. More than needing food to sustain him, David had to be reminded that God would fight his battles for him. Abigail continued her encouragement in verse 29 by saying, *"The lives of your enemies He [God] shall sling out, as from the pocket of a sling."* When we have favor in the sight of the Lord, it will often manifest itself in the form of encouragement and give us a fresh boost of confidence when all hope seems to be lost!

Nabal's response to his wife's generosity could have been predicted. He became so totally possessed by his anger that *"his heart died within him, and he became like a stone"* (v. 37). Ten days later, David was completely avenged when *"the Lord struck Nabal, and he died"* (v. 38). God knows how to take care of our enemies; we don't need to be concerned with them!

David remembered Abigail's gestures of kindness, and when Nabal died, he took the opportunity to return the blessing of favor to her. David sent for Abigail, and she became his wife. This was a particular period of David's life when he desperately needed all of the encouragement and confidence he could get. Based upon his first meeting with Abigail, he knew that she would do her best to bolster a discouraged spirit. Both Abigail and David were surrounded by a shield of God's favor, and they became a beautiful blessing to each other!

The name "Abigail" means "source of joy." I imagine that when God, her heavenly Father, looked down, He could have said, "Abigail, you truly are a source of joy. I am well pleased with you!"

Abigail knew how to respond with wisdom in difficult situations, and by doing so, she obtained favor and eventually became a queen of Israel. She reacted according to the Word of God: she blessed and fed her "enemies." If we react during times of trial with the same wisdom, and if we don't allow truth and mercy to forsake us, we will find favor with God and men (see Proverbs 3:3–4). What a promise!

Pour the living Word into your heart. Ask God to surround you with favor in precarious situations, especially ungodly ones. Some Christians say that God doesn't want us to have favor in the world. This particular kind of "religious thinking" is ridiculous and contrary to the Word of God. We should not only claim favor, we should *expect* favor wherever we go and with everyone whom we meet!

CHAPTER FIVE

# THE PRINCIPLES OF GODLY FAVOR

## SURRENDER

One of the things all of these great stories of favor have in common is surrender. Esther surrendered her very life to ask for an audience with the king. Her surrender brought about the salvation of her people throughout the Persian Empire.

Abigail surrendered to the wisdom of God and humbled herself before David in an act of reconciliation that saved her household and brought her favor and a place at David's side.

Ruth surrendered her homeland and family to care for Naomi. Part of that included taking Naomi's God — Yahweh — as her God. In doing all of this, she found favor with God and then with man, securing a blessing from her neighbors that put her name in the genealogy of Christ.

> **The spirit of this age, even among believers, seems to be: "No one is going to tell me what I can and can't do!"**

After some resistance, Naaman surrendered to the prophet and his instructions to dip in the Jordan River seven times. In doing so, his leprosy was healed. We can only surmise that his servant girl was also surrendered to the compassionate will of God, as she didn't hold back on her knowledge of Elisha and the miracles God could do through him.

There is also a great example of this in Luke 2:52. After describing the incident in which Jesus, at the age of 12, went missing and was found amazing all the teachers in the temple with His knowledge of the Word, Luke then says: *"Jesus increased in wisdom and stature, and in favor with God and men."* I have surely read that passage hundreds of times over the years, but I recently noticed something I'd never noticed before. It was hiding in plain sight in the previous verse: *"Then He* (Jesus) *went down with them* (his parents) *and came to Nazareth, and* **was subject to them** *..."* (v. 51). Please note the phrase I put in bold. It means Jesus submitted to His parents. He wasn't rebellious, stubborn, or willful. Even though He was the Son of God, He yielded to their earthly authority.

Think about it. Right before we learn that Jesus was growing in favor with God and men, we learn that He stayed in submission to His parents' authority. I don't think that's a coincidence! Yielding to authority — both heavenly and earthly — produces favor. Unfortunately, submitting to authority has fallen out of style. The spirit of this age, even among believers, seems to be: "No one is going to tell me what I can and can't do!" I believe this is why so many of God's people don't experience all the favor God wants to place upon their lives. They don't yield to the Holy Spirit when He prompts them, and they refuse to submit to any earthly authority.

As you might guess, I have a strong personality and strong opinions, but I learned early on in my life that when I yielded to Wally's leadership — when I chose to bless and honor him instead of rebelliously fighting him — I enjoyed lots and lots of favor with my husband and God. Do you want favor? Yielding to God and submitting to proper authority will bring it to you. It did in Jesus's life, and I've seen it do the same in mine!

> **We have a big God, and He can give us favor *and* help us keep our attitudes right when we surrender to His will.**

Now, part of surrendering to God includes your attitude. I remember one time when I went to Oakland, California, with two of my staff members, Pat and Mark. We got on the plane, and their seats were all the way at the back, and Pat grumbled to Mark, "Why is it we always get stuck at the back?"

Mark replied, "Well, maybe God has a purpose."

So, they sat down, and a woman came and sat in the seat across the aisle from them. They began to visit with her, and eventually, they led her to Christ! When we got off the plane, I got off early because I had a seat closer to the front. I was waiting for Pat and Mark, and here comes this woman with them, just radiant, who had received the Lord in the back of the plane! We have a big God, and He can give us favor *and* help us keep our attitudes right when we surrender to His will.

## PRAY FOR FAVOR

Next, you need to pray for favor. You also need to speak it and proclaim it. Some years ago, when Joel Osteen took over Lakewood Church, he invited me to come on a Sunday morning and speak. Afterwards, we had dinner with a group of people, and he said to me, "You know, Marilyn, really, I don't have a Bible background in the sense of Bible school. I don't have experience, and here I am stepping into this place. So, my greatest prayer is that Victoria and I will have favor."

Well, that prayer has really worked. Joel and Victoria were invited to meet with President Obama once, along with a lot of other people, and as they were standing in a receiving line, President Obama came to Joel and said, "Oh, Joel Osteen, come here, Michelle. We watch you on TV, Joel. And here's Victoria." That's favor, but that's not accidental. That came through prayer.

**But if I have favor with God,
He can give me favor with people.**

Now if Joel had said that day, "Well, you know, I'm stepping into big shoes. My father was so popular. He did so well. I just don't know if I can do this. What if, when I stand up there to preach, people don't like me? I just don't know if this is going to work." Do you think he would've had so much favor? No, he wouldn't have. He prayed for favor.

Now, does God love Joel Osteen more than you? No. Does he love you? Yes. Does he want you to have favor? Yes. Do *you* want to have favor? Then you must pray for it and proclaim it. I have three Scriptures below that I want you to proclaim over your life (there are more verses at the end of the book as well).

These are Scriptures that I have prayed over my life again and again and again:

# THE PRINCIPLES OF GODLY FAVOR

*"You have granted me life and favor,*
*And Your care has preserved*
*my spirit."* (JOB 10:12)

*For You, O Lord, will bless the righteous;*
*With favor You will surround him as with*
*a shield.* (PSALM 5:12)

*Let not mercy and truth forsake you;*
*Bind them around your neck,*
*Write them on the tablet of your heart,*
*And so find favor and high esteem in the sight*
*of God and man.* (PROVERBS 3:3–4)

## FAVOR HAS A PROCESS

I want you to look at the order that's found in the verse we just looked at: "*. . . so find favor and high esteem in the sight of God and man*" (Proverbs 3:4). First, we have favor with God, and then we have favor with man (people). Remember the story of Jesus as a little boy at the temple in Luke 2:52? It also has this same order. "*Jesus increased . . . in favor with God and men.*"

Usually, when I think of favor, I think of favor with people. But if I have favor with God, He can give me favor with people. When we're just looking for our own favor for our own purpose, and it isn't a godly purpose, then that's temporary favor. That's not the kind of favor we should be looking for. I remember when I was growing up, I wanted to look nice and smell good because I wanted to have favor with the guys in my class. I wanted them to ask me to the dance. I can't say that I wanted favor with man and God, I just really wanted favor with good-looking guys. But Proverbs 31:30 says, *"Charm is deceitful and beauty is passing, but a woman who fears the* Lord, *she shall be praised."*

You can look nice and smell good, but that's temporary. If you fear God and receive God's favor, you can have favor all your life. You can have favor when you're young, you can have favor in your middle age, and you can have favor in your old age. That's God's favor. The fear of the Lord and the favor that comes with it is not deceitful or temporary. God's favor is eternal.

# CHAPTER SIX

# THE BENEFITS OF GODLY FAVOR

## PURPOSE AND POWER

When God opens doors of favor, there is always a purpose. Ruth's favor saved her family lineage and put their names in the genealogy of Christ. The servant girl's favor brought healing to her master. Esther's favor saved all of the Jews living in Persia. Abigail's favor changed the outcome of a major conflict that could have brought death to her entire household.

God's purpose is always much bigger than you could ever anticipate or dream. God has a purpose for everyone reading this book. Nobody is an accident because we're all made in the image of God. So, when God begins to move in your life and give you favor, know that He has a purpose for your favor. He gives favor not just to bless you or make people like you. It's not just to make you feel warm and good. He's got a powerful, long-term purpose for that favor. Even in your smallest circumstance, God could be cooking up something that has a purpose far beyond what you can imagine or expect.

> **In your smallest circumstance, God could be cooking up something that has a purpose far beyond what you can imagine or expect.**

One time, God gave me favor with Joyce Meyer. Many years ago, before she was on radio, I went to a church to speak and raise money for the sanctuary they had just built. I was sitting on the front row, with a couple behind me. This woman touched me and said, "I know you're on radio and that you're going on television now." Then she said, "I would like to go on radio. Could you pray for me and my husband?"

I said, "Yes, what is your name?"

She replied, "My name is Joyce Meyer."

I never dreamed what a great ministry that would be, but God gave me favor with her, which gave me the opportunity to sow into her ministry through prayer. Many times, Joyce has sent large gifts to my ministry. Isn't that cool? But did I ever dream that financial blessing would come to me in that kind of situation? So, that's what I'm saying to you. In your smallest circumstance, God could be cooking up something that has a purpose far beyond what you can imagine or expect. You could lead someone to the Lord. You could heal the sick. Who knows what prayer you're going to pray that's going to turn somebody's life around? Who knows how big the purpose could be? You might not have a clue, but if you will submit to God and proclaim what He says, God's purpose will start to come to pass, and his power will be released. There's tremendous power in favor, and it takes power to accomplish God's purpose.

If you are liked by people in a certain place — in a nail shop, on an airplane — and you talk to those people, there is power in that. Favor opens doors with people.

I don't know about you, but I don't like to confront people because I think they won't like me afterwards. But Proverbs 28:23 says, *"He who rebukes a man will find more favor afterward than he who flatters with the tongue."* If you flatter people, in the end, it doesn't pay. But if you're honest with people — not ugly, but honest — in the end, it will bring favor.

I once had a good friend who was a very successful pastor. But even though he told me I was his spiritual mother, I never felt I could openly speak to him. However, I saw some things that I thought he was getting a little out of sync on. At the time, he had probably one of the biggest churches in our nation, so I was very concerned, but I didn't know what to do. Should I say, "I think you're out of sync"? Then he might say, "Well, I don't want you to be my mother anymore." I really prayed about it, and the Lord said to me, "Just hold on, keep claiming favor with him." One day, this friend said to me, "Now, since you're my mother, I want you to correct me." He gave me permission to speak into his life. Isn't that powerful?

Another time, a man said to me, "Marilyn, you know the Bible really well. You can pick up anything and just start preaching, but you need to hear from the Holy Spirit about what He wants you to preach." At first, I thought, *Oh be quiet. I know what I'm doing!* But it was true. I needed to hear that from him, and that man has great favor with me now.

## PROTECTION

Unfortunately, we can't gain favor with everyone. But I believe favor can bring you protection from people who despise you, are out to hurt you, or even want to kill you. Remember, Psalm 5:12 says, *"For You, O Lord, will bless the righteous; with favor You will surround him as with a shield."* When you have favor, God shields you.

I don't know why God would take me to Islamic countries in such dangerous times. I also don't know why God put it on my heart to go into the Gaza Strip. Gaza has 2 million people, and it's a very dangerous place. It is often on the news because of the conflicts between Israelis and Palestinians. But I had that region on my heart for years — I wanted to share the love of Jesus with them and find out how we could help the people in that area. In 2009, God gave me the opportunity to go into Gaza Strip with two of my ministry directors, Stephen and Joe. There was a very tall concrete wall built all the way around Gaza, and we could only get in through the Israeli stations. We all had the required paperwork, but after a couple of hours, only Stephen was let through. They didn't want someone (particularly a well-known Christian who's on television) to come in and get shot. They wanted to protect me and getting shot would be bad advertising. So, our guide told Joe and me, "They're not going to let you in. I'll take you to see some other places."

> **I had favor because they deserved to hear about Jesus. If they don't want Him, they can make that choice. But they can never stand before God and say, "Nobody told me."**

I responded and said, "I don't want to see any place else. I'm going to stay here because I'm going to go in."

"Well, they're not going to let you in." He continued, "I've called my uncle. He's over all this. It's not going to happen."

I said, "It's going to happen." Joe and I sat in a little hut near the checkpoint, confessing the Word of God. At two o'clock, it happened. I was let in! Joe was not allowed through, so I went in alone, but I had two angels beside me. Hallelujah! I walked one mile down a dirt road and through various checkpoints, which took about two hours. Finally, I was able to meet with Steven, an imam, a Christian minister, and a Greek Orthodox minister. Miraculously, they all agreed to have tea together with us so that we could find out the needs of Gaza and what we could do that would help the people most. Obviously, we weren't killed, and we crossed back over the border into Israel later that afternoon.

That short trip into the Gaza Strip took so much favor — favor with Hamas (the militant, fundamentalist organization that rules Gaza), favor at each checkpoint, and favor with the imam and two ministers. I had favor because they deserved to hear about Jesus. If they don't want Him, they can make that choice. But they can never stand before God and say, "Nobody told me." They can say instead, "Some crazy old lady from Denver, Colorado, wouldn't give up on us."

## PROVISION

So, we have favor, we have a purpose for that favor, we have power, and we have protection. We also have one more thing: provision.

Did you know favor can bring abundant provision? Psalm 35:27 says, *"Let them shout for joy and be glad, who favor my righteous cause; and let them say continually, 'Let the LORD be magnified, who has pleasure in the prosperity of His servant.'"* Also, in retelling some of the history of Israel, Psalm 44:3 states, *"For they did not gain possession of the land by their own sword, nor did their own arm save them; but it was Your right hand, Your arm, and the light of Your countenance, because You favored them."*

Let me give you a testimony of financial favor. When Wally and I started our church, we only had 22 people attend, but the church began to grow, and we got up to 70 or 80 people. Eighty people aren't really enough to support a young couple. Wally and I didn't have secular jobs, but God took care of us. I was invited to be in a vitamin business, so I prayed about it, and the Lord really dealt with me. He said, "I'll lead you in, and I'll lead you out. I'll tell you when to get in and when to get out, and I will prosper you." Every day I gave about an hour of time to this business. Well, in the first few years, I made over $35,000. This was well over 50 years ago, so that was a lot of money at that time. What did I do with it? I bought the house that we lived in for 32 years. God gave me such favor. He blessed and prospered me. But when He said, "It's time to leave," I left.

A woman said to me one time, "You know, you could make your husband unhappy because you make more money than he does."

Wally's response? "Don't believe her."

Daily, I claimed favor with people, and God blessed me and prospered my vitamin business. He will do the same with you! Just remember to surrender to His will. Let Him lead you in and let Him lead you out.

Now, the provision of favor is more than just financial. It can bring all sorts of things:

- **Turn-arounds:** *"For His anger is but for a moment, His favor is for life; weeping may endure for a night, but joy comes in the morning"* (Psalm 30:5). Regardless of your circumstances, seek God's favor, and your great reward of joy will come, because He has promised it.

- **Mercy and truth:** *"Let not mercy and truth forsake you; bind them around your neck, write them on the tablet of your heart, and so find favor and high esteem in the sight of God and man"* (Proverbs 3:3–4). Are there people you don't like? Are you judgmental? If you want favor, you must be merciful.

- **Good understanding:** *"Good understanding gains favor, but the way of the unfaithful is hard"* (Proverbs 13:15). Good understanding comes from reading the Bible. The Word will help you know what God says about circumstances and people. When you know what God says and do what He says, you will have favor.

- **Increase:** When you align your life to the Word of God, favor will follow you because you are in line with God's principles.

## THE BENEFITS OF GODLY FAVOR

*"So continuing daily with one accord in the temple, and breaking bread from house to house, they ate their food with gladness and simplicity of heart, praising God and having favor with all the people. And the Lord added to the church daily those who were being saved"* (Acts 2:46–47).

Do you remember, back in chapter two, how I took note of the special roles which servants played in Naaman's story? There was a reason for that. They illustrated the principles and benefits of godly favor in significant ways.

After Gehazi, Elisha's servant, heard that his master had refused to accept payment from Naaman for his healing, he ran after Naaman, saying that Elisha had changed his mind concerning acceptance of the treasure. Why do you think that Elisha refused the generous gift of wealth in the first place? No doubt, Gehazi wondered the same thing. Elisha was willing to give God alone the glory for the miraculous healing of Naaman. He didn't try to profit by the precious gift which God had entrusted to him.

Gehazi followed after Naaman, knowing it would be against Elisha's will. He lied to Naaman and convinced him that his master had changed his mind about receiving payment. When Gehazi returned to Elisha, his master recognized his deceit and asked:

> *"Where did you go, Gehazi?" And he said, "Your servant did not go anywhere." Then he said to him, "Did not my heart go with you when the man turned back from his chariot to meet you? Is it time to receive money and to receive clothing, olive groves and vineyards, sheep and oxen, male and female servants? Therefore the leprosy of Naaman shall cling to you and your descendants forever."*
> (2 KINGS 5:25–27)

Although Gehazi had spent time living with Elisha, he didn't profit much from the experience because he went after wealth and tried to deceive his master. Instead of submitting to God and his master, Gehazi let the wrong thing control him and ended up in very difficult circumstances. The Bible adamantly teaches that *"the wages of sin is death, but the gift of God is eternal life in Christ Jesus our Lord"* (Romans 6:23).

The other important servant in this story, our nameless little maid, wrapped understanding, mercy, and truth around her spirit and, I believe, changed the course of historic events in both Syria and Israel. Gehazi, on the other hand, would not allow mercy and truth to be found in him, and as a result, he lost favor with God and man.

## STAND ON THE WORD OF GOD

Do you realize how important it is to spend time reading and meditating on the Word? When we surround ourselves with the favor of God's Word, we can confidently step out in faith and change situations around us. The wisdom of the Word in your spirit will give you favor, regardless of the circumstances which may confront you or the people whom you may meet. Again, remember Psalm 5:12, *"For You, O Lord, will bless the righteous; with favor You will surround him as with a shield."* You have an invisible shield of favor surrounding you.

Whenever you are in a state of doubt, fear, or anxiety, remind God of His promise: *"But You, O Lord, are a shield for me, my glory and the One who lifts up my head"* (Psalm 3:3). Likewise, Hebrews 10:35 tells us to *"not cast away your confidence, which has great reward."* Always lift your head high above all circumstances. You are wearing His glorious crown of divine favor.

Many times, we experience deep levels of grief and frustration, but if we hold fast to God's promises, any situation can be altered! Hebrews 10:23 commands us to *"hold fast the confession of our hope without wavering, for He who promised is faithful."*

David understood the awesome power of favor because in Psalm 30 he writes, *"Lord, by Your favor You have made my mountain stand strong...."* (v. 7). If God's favor is powerful enough to make a mountain stand, it is definitely strong enough to hold you up, no matter how heavy the pressures may be which come against you! Always remember that He is *"upholding all things by the word of His power"* (Hebrews 1:3). If you are standing on His Word, you can count on Him to uphold all the things in your life and give you wide open doors of favor. Hallelujah!

## APPENDIX A

# PRAYERS FOR FAVOR

The prayers below are designed to follow the pages you just read. Acknowledge your need for favor in a particular area, confess any sin, and surrender to God's process and plan. Then proclaim His Word over that area in your life and thank Him for the purpose, power, protection, and provision that will accompany the favor you receive.

*Feel free to personalize . . .*

- The family prayer with the names of your family members.

- The healing prayer with the areas where you need healing.
- The prayer for your nation, with the names of your city, state, country, etc.
- The prayer over circumstances with the specific situation in which you need favor.

**Pray Favor for Your Family:**

Dear heavenly Father, I thank you for new beginnings of favor for my family. Like Naomi, I haven't always made the right decisions or had the right attitudes, but I ask for your forgiveness in the areas where I have fallen short. On behalf of my family, I surrender to your authority, plan, and purpose for us. I proclaim John 15:16 over my family today: that you have chosen us to go and bear fruit, and that the fruit will remain. I pray that you will give my family the favor we need to be fruitful in our jobs, schools, home lives, and any other circumstances that we encounter. I thank you for the power, protection, and provision that accompany our divine favor. I also praise you for all we will see you accomplish through us that will affect not just today but the future as well. In Jesus's name, amen.

**Scriptures to pray over your family:**

> *"You did not choose Me, but I chose you and appointed you that you should go and bear fruit, and that your fruit should remain, that whatever you ask the Father in My name He may give you."* (JOHN 15:16)

> *"Blessing I will bless you, and multiplying I will multiply your descendants as the stars of the heaven and as the sand which is on the seashore; and your descendants shall possess the gate of their enemies. In your seed all the nations of the earth shall be blessed, because you have obeyed My voice."* (GENESIS 22:17–18)

> *Unless the LORD builds the house,*
> *They labor in vain who build it;*
> *Unless the LORD guards the city,*

*The watchman stays awake in vain.*
(PSALM 127:1)

*Behold, children are a heritage from the* L<small>ORD</small>,
*The fruit of the womb is a reward.* (PSALM 127:3)

*Your wife shall be like a fruitful vine*
*In the very heart of your house,*
*Your children like olive plants*
*All around your table.* (PSALM 128:3)

*The wicked are overthrown and are no more,*
*But the house of the righteous will stand.*
(PROVERBS 12:7)

*"Believe on the Lord Jesus Christ, and you will be saved, you and your household."* (ACTS 16:31)

*For the unbelieving husband is sanctified by the wife, and the unbelieving wife is sanctified by the husband; otherwise your children would be unclean, but now they are holy.*
(1 CORINTHIANS 7:14)

## Pray Favor for Your Health:

Dear heavenly Father, I'm asking you to give me favor for my health. Like Naaman, I haven't always submitted to doing what you've told me to do, and I ask for your forgiveness. Today, I submit to your authority, purpose, and plan for my health and healing. I proclaim, according to your Word, that if I cry out to you, you will heal me and deliver me from my afflictions. I know that by the stripes of Jesus I am healed. I praise you for the power, protection, and provision that your favor will give me over my health in the name of Jesus. Amen.

***Scriptures to pray over your health:***

> O LORD my God, I cried out to You,
> And You healed me. (PSALM 30:2)

> Many are the afflictions of the righteous,
> But the LORD delivers him out of them all.
> (PSALM 34:19)

*He sent His word and healed them,*
*And delivered them from their destructions.*
(PSALM 107:20)

*He heals the brokenhearted*
*And binds up their wounds.* (PSALM 147:3)

*But He was wounded for our transgressions,*
*He was bruised for our iniquities;*
*The chastisement for our peace was upon Him,*
*And by His stripes we are healed.* (ISAIAH 53:5)

*Heal me, O LORD, and I shall be healed;*
*Save me, and I shall be saved,*
*For You are my praise.* (JEREMIAH 17:14)

*[JESUS] Himself bore our sins in His own body on the tree, that we, having died to sins, might live for righteousness — by whose stripes you were healed.* (1 PETER 2:24)

## Pray Favor for Your Nation:

Dear heavenly Father, like Esther, I feel that I have been called "for such a time as this." My nation really needs your favor right now. On behalf of my nation, I repent for the things we have done that have not been pleasing to you. I ask for your forgiveness, and I pray that you will reveal to me anything other than prayer that I need to do to win my nation for you. I surrender to the process and purpose you have for me and my nation. Right now, I proclaim Psalm 2:8, *"Ask of Me, and I will give You the nations for Your inheritance, and the ends of the earth for Your possession."* I'm asking for my nation to be part of the inheritance I have through Jesus, your son. I thank you in advance for the miraculous power, protection, and provision of favor I'm going to see released on me and my nation in the days to come. In Jesus's name, amen.

**Scriptures to pray over your nation:**

> "Be strong and of good courage, do not fear nor be afraid of them; for the LORD your God, He is the One who goes with you. He will not leave you nor forsake you." (DEUTERONOMY 31:6)

> "Ask of Me, and I will give You
> The nations for Your inheritance,
> And the ends of the earth for Your possession."
> (PSALM 2:8)

> The fruit of the righteous is a tree of life,
> And he who wins souls is wise. (PROVERBS 11:30)

> Commit your works to the LORD,
> And your thoughts will be established.
> (PROVERBS 16:3)

> "Go therefore and make disciples of all the nations, baptizing them in the name of the Father and of the Son and of the Holy Spirit,

*teaching them to observe all things that I have commanded you; and lo, I am with you always, even to the end of the age."* (MATTHEW 28:19–20)

*"You did not choose Me, but I chose you and appointed you that you should go and bear fruit, and that your fruit should remain, that whatever you ask the Father in My name He may give you."* (JOHN 15:16)

*But you are a chosen generation, a royal priesthood, a holy nation, His own special people, that you may proclaim the praises of Him who called you out of darkness into His marvelous light.* (1 PETER 2:9)

## Pray Favor for Your Circumstances

Dear heavenly Father, like Abigail, I need your wisdom and favor over the situation I am in right now. I come boldly to your throne of grace to obtain mercy and grace. If I have fallen short in any area, I confess that sin to you right now and ask for your forgiveness. I surrender this situation into your hands and proclaim that I am more than a conqueror through Christ Jesus. I know that you will work this situation for good because I am called according to your purpose, and you have a purpose even in this. I thank you for that purpose and praise you for the power, protection, and provision that will accompany your divine favor in this circumstance. In Jesus's name I pray, amen.

**Scriptures to pray over your circumstances:**

> *I will instruct you and teach you in the way*
> *    you should go;*
> *I will guide you with My eye.* (PSALM 32:8)

> *You shall not be afraid of the terror by night,*
> *Nor of the arrow that flies by day,*
> *Nor of the pestilence that walks in darkness,*
> *Nor of the destruction that lays waste*
> *    at noonday.*
> *A thousand may fall at your side,*
> *And ten thousand at your right hand;*
> *But it shall not come near you.* (PSALM 91:5–7)

"*I will give you the keys of the kingdom of heaven, and whatever you bind on earth will be bound in heaven, and whatever you loose on earth will be loosed in heaven.*" (MATTHEW 16:19)

*And we know that all things work together for good to those who love God, to those who are the called according to His purpose.*
(ROMANS 8:28)

*Yet in all these things we are more than conquerors through Him who loved us.*
(ROMANS 8:37)

*May He who supplies seed to the sower, and bread for food, supply and multiply the seed you have sown and increase the fruits of your righteousness, while you are enriched in everything for all liberality, which causes thanksgiving through us to God.*
(2 CORINTHIANS 9:10–11)

*My brethren, count it all joy when you fall into various trials, knowing that the testing of your faith produces patience. But let patience have its perfect work, that you may be perfect and complete, lacking nothing.* (JAMES 1:2–4)

*Let us therefore come boldly to the throne of grace, that we may obtain mercy and find grace to help in time of need.* (HEBREWS 4:16)

*Therefore humble yourselves under the mighty hand of God, that He may exalt you in due time, casting all your care upon Him, for He cares for you.* (1 PETER 5:6–7)

**APPENDIX B**

# SCRIPTURES ON FAVOR

The following Scriptures are intended to prove that God will produce favor in your life. Meditate upon these Scriptures and memorize them until they penetrate deep down into your spirit. If you plant them in your heart now, when you are in a time of need, they will be firmly rooted, and you will be able to stand upon them. I just love these verses, and I believe you will, too!

> "You have granted me life and favor,
> And Your care has preserved my spirit."
> (JOB 10:12)

*For You, O* Lord, *will bless the righteous;*
*With favor You will surround him as with a shield.*
(PSALM 5:12)

*For His anger is but for a moment,*
*His favor is for life;*
*Weeping may endure for a night,*
*But joy comes in the morning.* (PSALM 30:5)

*Let them shout for joy and be glad,*
*Who favor my righteous cause;*
*And let them say continually,*
*"Let the* Lord *be magnified,*
*Who has pleasure in the prosperity of His servant."*
(PSALM 35:27)

*By this I know that You favor me, because*
*my enemy does not triumph over me.*
(PSALM 41:11, MEV)

*For they did not gain possession of the land*
     *by their own sword,*
*Nor did their own arm save them;*

## SCRIPTURES ON FAVOR

*But it was Your right hand, Your arm,*
  *and the light of Your countenance,*
*Because You favored them.* (PSALM 44:3)

*For the* LORD *God is a sun and shield;*
  *the* LORD *bestows favor and honor;*
*no good thing does he withhold*
  *from those whose walk is blameless.*
(PSALM 84:11, NIV)

*For You are the glory of their strength,*
*And in Your favor our horn is exalted.*
(PSALM 89:17)

*May the favor of the Lord our God rest on us;*
*establish the work of our hands for us —*
  *yes, establish the work of our hands.*
(PSALM 90:17, NIV)

*Remember me, O Lord, with the favor*
  *You have toward Your people.*
*Oh, visit me with Your salvation.*
*That I may see the benefit of Your chosen ones,*

*That I may rejoice in the gladness of*
  *Your nation,*
*That I may glory with Your inheritance.*
(PSALM 106:4–5)

*Let not mercy and truth forsake you;*
*Bind them around your neck,*
*Write them on the tablet of your heart,*
*And so find favor and high esteem*
*In the sight of God and man.* (PROVERBS 3:3–4)

*He who earnestly seeks good finds favor,*
*But trouble will come to him who seeks evil.*
(PROVERBS 11:27)

*A good man obtains favor from the* L<small>ORD</small>,
*But a man of wicked intentions He will condemn.* (PROVERBS 12:2)

*Good understanding gains favor,*
*But the way of the unfaithful is hard.*
(PROVERBS 13:15)

## SCRIPTURES ON FAVOR

*Fools mock at sin,*
*But among the upright there is favor.*
(PROVERBS 14:9)

*In the light of the king's face is life,*
*And his favor is like a cloud of the latter rain.*
(PROVERBS 16:15)

*He who finds a wife finds a good thing,*
*And obtains favor from the* L`ORD`.
(PROVERBS 18:22)

*A good name is to be chosen rather*
*than great riches,*
*Loving favor rather than silver and gold.*
(PROVERBS 22:1)

*"These are the ones I look on with favor:*
*those who are humble and contrite in spirit,*
*and who tremble at my word."* (ISAIAH 66:2, NIV)

*So continuing daily with one accord in the*
*temple, and breaking bread from house to*
*house, they ate their food with gladness and*

*simplicity of heart, praising God and having favor with all the people. And the Lord added to the church daily those who were being saved.*
(ACTS 2:46–47)

*For he who serves Christ in these things is acceptable to God and approved by men.*
(ROMANS 14:18)

# END NOTES

## A Note from Marilyn
Surround means crown: James Strong, *The New Strong's Complete Dictionary of Bible Words*, (1996), s.v. "Atar."

Eight is the number of new beginnings: John Ashcraft, "What Is the Significance of Biblical Numerology?" Updated April 15, 2021. Christianity.com.

https://www.christianity.com/wiki/christian-terms/what-is-the-significance-of-biblical-numerology.html.

## Chapter One
Becoming a kinsman-redeemer: "Dictionary of Bible Themes – 7388 Kinsman-Redeemer." BibleGateway.com. https://www.biblegateway.com/resources/dictionary-of-bible-themes/7388-kinsman-redeemer.

## Chapter Three

Expose herself indecently: Robert Jamieson, "Commentary on Esther 1." Blue Letter Bible. https://www.blueletterbible.org/Comm/jfb/Est/Est_001.cfm.

He had made a big mistake: Flavius Josephus, *Josephus: The Complete Works*. Christian Classics Ethereal Library. https://www.ccel.org/ccel/j/josephus/complete/cache/complete.pdf.

Esther means star: Mike Campbell, "Esther." Updated May 29, 2020. Behind the Name. https://www.behindthename.com/name/esther.

Providence means forethought of care and supply: James Strong, *The New Strong's Complete Dictionary of Bible Words*, (1996), s.v. "Pronoia."

## Chapter Four

Nabal means folly: James Strong, *The New Strong's Complete Dictionary of Bible Words*, (1996), s.v. "Nabal."

Rest means to be quiet or still: James Strong, *The New Strong's Complete Dictionary of Bible Words*, (1996), s.v. "Shaqat."

Abigail means source of joy: James Strong, *The New Strong's Complete Dictionary of Bible Words*, (1996), s.v. "Abigail."

# FAVOR FOREVER

You can have divine favor and Jesus's joy, peace, protection, and provision in your life starting today. You can also know for sure that you will have life after death in heaven.

God sent Jesus Christ to be the Savior of the world. First Timothy 2:5–6 says, *"For there is one God and one Mediator between God and men, the Man Christ Jesus, who gave Himself a ransom for all."*

The Bible tells us how we can receive Jesus as Savior:

*If you confess with your mouth the Lord Jesus and believe in your heart that God has raised Him from the dead, you will be saved.*

*For with the heart one believes unto righteousness, and with the mouth confession is made unto salvation.* (ROMANS 10:9–10)

Would you like to begin a personal relationship with God and Jesus right now? You can! Simply pray this prayer in sincerity:

*Heavenly Father, I acknowledge that I need your help. I am not able to change my life or circumstances through my own efforts. I know that I have made some wrong decisions in my life, and at this moment, I turn away from those ways of thinking and acting. I believe you have provided a way for me through Jesus to receive your blessings and help in my life. Right now, I believe and confess Jesus as my Lord and Savior. I ask Jesus to come into my heart and give me a new life, by your Spirit. I thank you for saving me, and I ask for your grace and mercy in my life. I pray this in Jesus's name. Amen.*

*If you just prayed to make Jesus your Lord, we want to know!*

*Please call us today — toll free — at 888-637-4545.*

*We will pray for you and send you a special gift to help you in your new life with Christ.*

# ABOUT MARILYN

Encouraging, optimistic, always upbeat and energetic, even in her later years, Marilyn Hickey actively ministers internationally. As founder and president of *Marilyn & Sarah Ministries*, a non-profit ministry and humanitarian organization based in Denver, Colorado, Marilyn has traveled to over 140 countries and has impacted many nations around the world — from disaster relief efforts in Haiti, Indonesia, and Pakistan to providing food for the hungry in Mexico, Costa Rica, Russia, and the Philippines.

Her legacy includes significant ministry in Islamic countries. In 2016, over one million people attended her healing meeting in Karachi, Pakistan.

Marilyn has held audiences with government leaders and heads of state all over the world. She was the first woman to join the board of directors for Dr. David Yonggi Cho (founder of the world's largest congregation, Yoido Full Gospel Church in South Korea).

Along with her daughter, pastor Sarah Bowling, she co-hosts the daily television program, *Today with Marilyn & Sarah*, which is broadcast globally in nearly 200 countries with a potential viewing audience of over 2 billion households worldwide. Marilyn has also authored over 100 publications.

She and her late husband, Wallace, were married over 50 years and have two children and five grandchildren. Marilyn holds a Bachelor of Arts in Collective Foreign Languages from the University of Northern Colorado and an Honorary Doctor of Divinity from Oral Roberts University.

In 2015, Marilyn was honored at Oral Roberts University with the prestigious Lifetime Global Achievement Award. This award recognizes individuals, or organizations, that have made a significant impact in the history of ORU and around the world. In 2019, Marilyn also received an International

Lifetime Peace Award from the Grand Imam and President of Pakistan.

In 2021, Marilyn was honored with two awards from the Assemblies of God Theological Seminary: The Pillar of Faith Award in acknowledgment of her worldwide impact on the church through biblical teaching and sustainable healing ministry; and the Smith Wigglesworth Award, given on behalf of the entire Assemblies of God fellowship in acknowledgment of her decades of service worldwide.

Marilyn's greatest passion and desire is to continue being a bridge-builder in countries around the world, and she shows no signs of stopping.

## TO LEARN MORE ABOUT MARILYN & SARAH MINISTRIES, VISIT:

**Marilyn & Sarah Ministries: marilynandsarah.org**
Check out our free downloads that include Bible reading plans, teaching notes, inspirational graphics, spiritual self-assessments, and lists of verses based on topic.

**Online Master Classes: mentoredbymarilyn.org**
Marilyn is passing her mantle on to you! Through her anointed master classes, you will be mentored in strategic areas that will take you to the next level of victory and fulfillment in your life and ministry. This is an incredible opportunity to mentored by Marilyn!

**Connect with Marilyn:**

- MarilynHickeyMinistries
- MarilynandSarah
- MarilynHickeyMinistries
- MarilynHickeyMinistries